CENYP

ACV 1872

D0406877

DISCARDED

| J
BIO

WRIGHT | Burleigh,
Robert.
    Into the
air : the
story of the
Wright
brothers' |

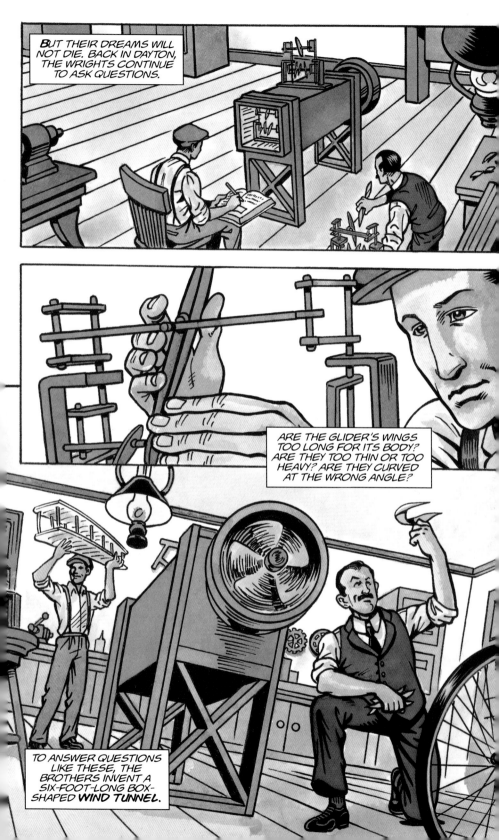

BUT THEIR DREAMS WILL NOT DIE. BACK IN DAYTON, THE WRIGHTS CONTINUE TO ASK QUESTIONS.

ARE THE GLIDER'S WINGS TOO LONG FOR ITS BODY? ARE THEY TOO THIN OR TOO HEAVY? ARE THEY CURVED AT THE WRONG ANGLE?

TO ANSWER QUESTIONS LIKE THESE, THE BROTHERS INVENT A SIX-FOOT-LONG BOX-SHAPED **WIND TUNNEL**.

THEY USE THE NEW FINDINGS TO CHANGE THE WEIGHT, SHAPE, AND ANGLES OF THE WINGS FOR THEIR 1902 GLIDER.

THIS WILL HELP US CONTROL TURNS EVEN BETTER.

I CAN'T WAIT TO TRY IT!

THE BROTHERS ALSO ADD AN IMPORTANT NEW FEATURE—A TAIL MADE OF SIDE-BY-SIDE VERTICAL FINS.

AS USUAL, THE BROTHERS MAKE EVERYTHING THEMSELVES.

HMMM, MAYBE I SHOULD MAKE MYSELF A NEW SUIT WHILE I'M AT IT. IF I CAN'T FLY, AT LEAST I CAN BE WELL DRESSED!

PREPARING ONCE MORE TO RETURN TO KITTY HAWK, THEY WONDER: WILL THE THIRD YEAR BE A CHARM?

HOW MANY MORE ATTEMPTS CAN THEY MAKE BEFORE THEY ARE FORCED TO ADMIT DEFEAT?

WITH KATHARINE'S HELP, THEY EVEN SEW THE COTTON WING COVERINGS.

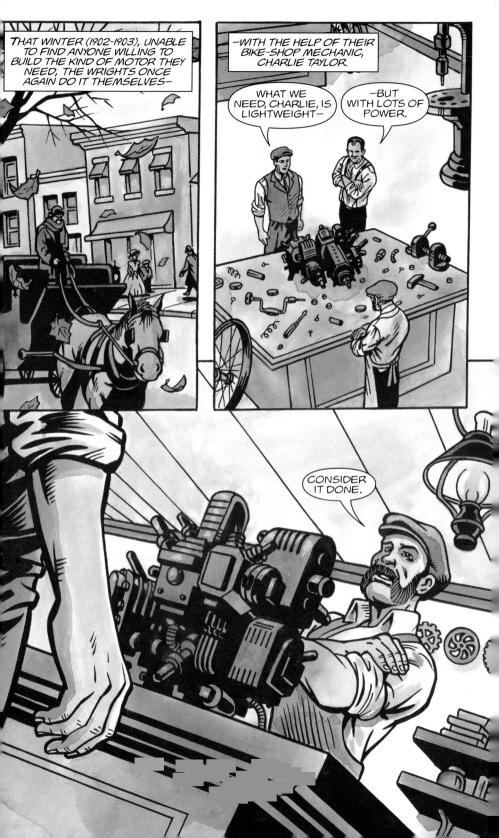

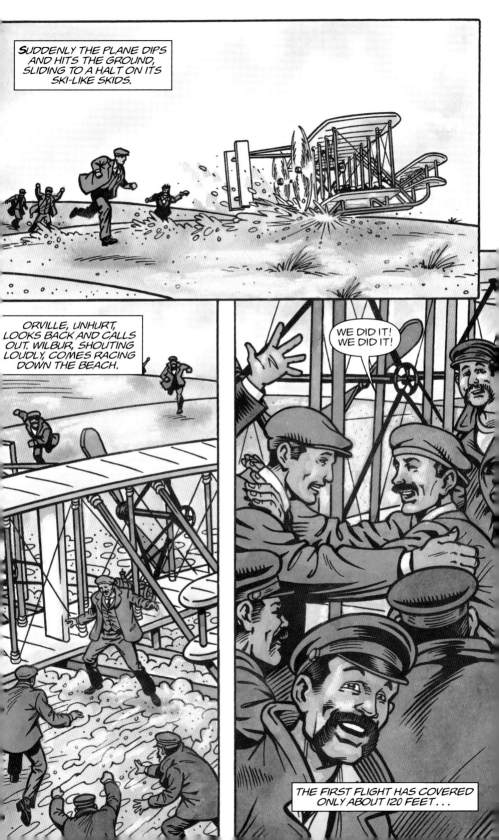

THAT AFTERNOON, THE WRIGHTS WALK INTO TOWN AND SEND A TELEGRAM. THEIR FATHER HAS GIVEN THEM A DOLLAR TO WIRE HOME, WHERE HE AND KATHARINE ANXIOUSLY AWAIT THE NEWS—

—WHICH ARRIVES WITH A FEW SLIGHT MISTAKES, INCLUDING THE INCORRECT TIME THE FLYER STAYED IN THE AIR.

TELEGRAM

success four flights thursday morning all against twenty one mile wind started from level with engine power alone average speed through air thirty one miles longest 57 seconds inform press home christmas

AFTERWORD

THE WRIGHT BROTHERS' STORY DID NOT END AT KITTY HAWK. AS THE BROTHERS WELL KNEW, THERE WAS MORE WORK TO BE DONE ON THE AIRPLANE. SOME OF THE PROBLEMS STILL TO BE RESOLVED INCLUDED MAKING THE TAKEOFF SIMPLER, LEARNING TO EXECUTE COMPLETE TURNS IN THE AIR, AND DESIGNING THE PLANE SO THAT THE PILOT COULD FLY SITTING UP. IN 1904 AND 1905, THE BROTHERS USED AN EMPTY PASTURE NEAR THEIR HOME IN DAYTON FOR MANY ADDITIONAL EXPERIMENTS AND TESTS.

MEANWHILE, ONLY SLOWLY DID PEOPLE IN THE UNITED STATES AND ABROAD BECOME AWARE OF THE WRIGHT BROTHERS AND THE IMPORTANCE OF THEIR INVENTION. FOR SEVERAL YEARS, THE AMERICAN GOVERNMENT SHOWED NO INTEREST IN THE WRIGHTS' FLYING MACHINE. FINALLY, IN 1908, THE BROTHERS WERE ABLE TO CONVINCE THE GOVERNMENT THAT FLIGHT WAS POSSIBLE AND USEFUL. DURING THE SAME YEAR, WILBUR WENT TO EUROPE AND GAVE A SERIES OF FLYING DEMONSTRATIONS THAT MADE HIM AND ORVILLE INSTANT CELEBRITIES.

WILBUR DIED OF AN ILLNESS IN 1912. BUT ORVILLE, WHO DIED IN 1948, LIVED TO SEE "THE AGE OF FLIGHT" EXPAND IN WAYS THAT HE AND HIS BROTHER NEVER FORESAW. TODAY THERE IS A SIXTY-FOOT-HIGH MONUMENT TO THE WRIGHT BROTHERS AT KILL DEVIL HILLS, NORTH CAROLINA. BUT PERHAPS THE REAL MONUMENTS TO THE VISION, COURAGE, AND DEDICATION OF WILBUR AND ORVILLE WRIGHT ARE THE AIRPLANES YOU SEE ABOVE YOU, FLYING BACK AND FORTH ACROSS THE COUNTRY, EVERY DAY.

ROBERT BURLEIGH HAS WRITTEN MANY BOOKS FOR CHILDREN, INCLUDING *FLIGHT: THE JOURNEY OF CHARLES LINDBERGH*, ILLUSTRATED BY MIKE WIMMER, WHICH RECEIVED THE ORBIS PICTUS AWARD FOR NONFICTION; AND *HOOPS*, ILLUSTRATED BY STEPHEN T. JOHNSON, A *BOOKLIST* EDITORS' CHOICE AND A *SCHOOL LIBRARY JOURNAL* BEST BOOK OF THE YEAR. MR. BURLEIGH LIVES WITH HIS WIFE IN CHICAGO, ILLINOIS.

BILL WYLIE HAS ILLUSTRATED MANY COMIC BOOKS, INCLUDING THE SECRET DEFENDERS SERIES AND SINGLE ISSUES OF NOMAD, NIGHTSTALKERS, AND NAMOR, ALL PUBLISHED BY MARVEL COMICS. MR. WYLIE LIVES WITH HIS WIFE IN BROOKLYN, NEW YORK. *INTO THE AIR* IS HIS FIRST CHILDREN'S BOOK.

For Judy and Steve "Moon" Myers, with love
—R. B.

To Mom and Dad
—B. W.

Text copyright © 2002 by Robert Burleigh
Illustrations copyright © 2002 by Bill Wylie

All rights reserved. No part of this publication may be reproduced or transmitted in
any form or by any means, electronic or mechanical, including photocopy, recording, or any
information storage and retrieval system, without permission in writing from the publisher.

Requests for permission to make copies of any part of the work should be
mailed to the following address: Permissions Department, Harcourt, Inc.,
6277 Sea Harbor Drive, Orlando, Florida 32887-6777.

www.HarcourtBooks.com

Silver Whistle is a trademark of Harcourt, Inc., registered
in the United States of America and/or other jurisdictions.

Library of Congress Cataloging-in-Publication Data
Burleigh, Robert.
Into the air: the story of the Wright brothers' first flight/
Robert Burleigh; illustrated by Bill Wylie.
p. cm.
"Silver Whistle."
1. Wright, Orville, 1871–1948—Juvenile literature.
2. Wright, Wilbur, 1867–1912—Juvenile literature. 3. Aeronautics—United States—
Biography–Juvenile literature. 4. Inventors—United States—Biography—
Juvenile literature. 5. Aeronautics—United States—History—Juvenile literature.
[1. Wright, Orville, 1871–1948. 2. Wright, Wilbur, 1867–1912.
3. Aeronautics—Biography. 4. Cartoons and comics.]
I. Wylie, Bill, ill. II. Title.
TL540.W7B87 2002
629.13'092'273—dc21 00-10857
ISBN 0-15-202492-1
ISBN 0-15-216803-6 (pb)

First edition
A C E G H F D B
A C E G H F D B (pb)

Printed in Singapore

The illustrations in this book were done in Luma dyes on card stock.
The display type and speech balloons were created by Ken Lopez.
The text type was set in WhizBang.
Color separations by Bright Arts Ltd., Hong Kong
Printed and bound by Tien Wah Press, Singapore
This book was printed on totally chlorine-free Nymolla Matte Art paper.
Production supervision by Sandra Grebenar and Pascha Gerlinger
Designed by Lydia D'moch